Wabi-Sabi

Tianna Maidment

Wabi-Sabi © 2022 Tianna Maidment

All rights reserved.

No part of this publication may be reproduced, stored in a retrieval system, or transmitted, in any form or by any means, electronic, mechanical, photocopying, recording or otherwise, without the prior written permission of the presenters.

Tianna Maidment asserts the moral right to be identified as author of this work.

Presentation by *BookLeaf Publishing*

Web: www.bookleafpub.com

E-mail: info@bookleafpub.com

ISBN: 9789357614030

First edition 2022

I dedicate this book to everyone out there who wake up in the same war as yesterday, to everyone whose minds tournament and tease.

You're not alone.

To overcome our darkness first we must make peace with it.

Our darkness does not and will never define us.

When our minds become a prison for our souls it's imperative to realise we've always had to key to set ourselves free.

ACKNOWLEDGEMENT

I thank BookLeaf Publishing for this opportunity.
#TheWriteAngle
I thank my English teachers, who instilled my love for writing, for providing me with a release.
I thank my teej, for everything.
<3 

PREFACE

Wabi-sabi, a Japanese term rooted in Zen Buddhism, a belief in which there is to be beauty appreciated in what is perceived to be imperfect. This book is an anthology of raw emotion.

Perception Is Not Actuality

They say you don't know what you've got until
you've lost it.
Now that I am gone I know who I am,
I never lost it.
You see I am not what I am said to be.
I am more than the image you have of me.
All these thoughts and emotions, I know I
probably shouldn't share it.
Still, I write for the chance to be heard for once.
Still, I write for the chance to be seen for once.
Still, I write for the chance to make a change for
once.
Your opinion of me does not define me,
Nor the way you see me.
I am who I am because of who you are.
So if you don't like me take a look at who you
are.
I know it's not fair to put the blame on any one
person.
For this sickness has been passed down behind
the curtain.
Regardless I remain unbothered.
I don't care who you think I am,
Because at least I know who I am.
I know I am not a perfect person,

But I know that I am a good person.
No one can take that away from me.
No thought, no place, no memory.

AGHHHHH

I want to run away.
I want to leave this place behind.
I want to get away from the pain,
From the demons that torture my mind.
I want to go where there's no end in sight,
I want it all to end.
It's a gift.
It's a curse.
I haven't decided yet.
All I know is that it really fucking hurts.
Have you ever questioned your own insanity?
Wondering what on Earth is this blasphemy!
I know this isn't the life for me.
I know this life isn't a reality.

I Refuse To Let This Be My Fate

They prostitute our souls,
To dispute our sins.
They downplay our goals,
Always tell us we can't win.
The things that make us human,
Merely thrown in the bin.
When replaced with machine,
Dispels humanity within.
We find ourselves barely alive,
In this time of confusion.
One can only hope for resolution,
During this downward movement.

How do they expect us to live in a world that's
ruined?
Given up on repairs, searching for a new one.
The television narrative slurs a daily illusion.
I refuse to be confined by the constitution.
Is there any solution or are we doomed to this
humanitarian pollution?
There is no life on mars.
There is no substitution.
This is our problem, there's no where to run,
No where to hide.

Fighting each other will only see to devolution
When the ash and smoke settle, and there
remains none,
Awake from the dead, then tell me who won.

Life Is Confined By The Barriers In Our Mind

I went for a walk to the Purple Tree.
I went to the tree just to see.
Just to see what life could be,
And what life could be, is up to me.
I went for a walk to the Purple Tree.

Time; An Overrated Social Construct

Time is scarce like a droplet in the desert.
Yet still we find ourselves caught up in the past
somehow.
Stuck worrying about the future so much that
we're missing the right now.
All that matters is what is happening in the
present moment.
How we create something in the passing of time.
Our lifetime is a mere blip in infinity.
It's up to us, to use our time efficiently.

Birth, Death, Afterbirth

If you believe this is the only plane of existence
then this will be it for you.
Only when you open your mind and see there's
more after death will you experience death for
what it is.
The word death itself is a human construct.
We invented words to capture communication.
What words lack is the ability to capture in full
depth.
An experience minimised to a comprehensive
manner.
No one knows what it is for certain the concept
of death.
After all, a corpse can't testify.
Scientific study show energy in consciousness.
A body, mind, and soul.
As energy cannot be created nor destroyed,
All who once were remain amongst the Spiritual
Plane.
It doesn't make sense any other way.
So hold on close to the ones you love,
You'll be together another day.

Stand Down Soldier

Ashamed of being in pain.
Ashamed of feeling insane.
The pointless fighting, constant crying.
Dying to live but only living to die.
What was born from darkness is now a comfort.
I don't understand what this has come to.
We're wasting precious time,
A finite band that wraps around life.
If time is the essence, then to wait is a crime.
Let's start right now.
Let's move out.
This head is cramped, time to face it.
There is no space for exasperation.
Take your friends on a nice vacation,
Leave me be for contemplation.
I want to see a nation of pain marching away.
Feels like a dream but maybe one day.
One day I'll say "I'm Okay" without hesitation.
On the highest hill, at a favoured destination.
I'm freeing my mind from this captivation.
The cell of the past unlocked and released.
The guards that once stood tall,
 f

  a

   l

    l

unnecessary,
They don't realise we're out of misery.
It's a safe place now, the rest is history.

Ignorance Isn't Acceptance

I never asked for this.
People can say it's a gift and not a curse,
But the truth is, it's hell on earth.
Of course that's what you'd say,
To make us feel better about being this way
How thoughtful of you.
How awful.
Constant lies that it'll be okay,
Is that still what you'd say if you read my brain?
Forget the darkest pages you've ever read.
The chapters of my life precisely stored away,
Haunting me, everyday.
Why was I born this way?
I long for the day I wake up dead.
I don't mean to sound morbid
For the concept of death
Is far easier to grasp than this torturous head.

Inhale 1,2,3. Exhale 1,2,3.

Okay one minute, a wreck the next.

An emotional whiplash.
So fast it could break a neck.

I can't

quite catch

my breath.

heavy, heavy chest.

I'm a mess. I'm a mess. I'm a mess. I'm a mess.
I'm a mess. I'm a mess.

FUCK!

Please show me what's next,

What's right and what's left.

Show me the light in this solemnly quest.

Inspiration In The Uninspired

If they say to write what you feel,
Then the heart is the pen.
The pages are a mirror of within,
The words are a reflection of skin.
And so these blank pages scare me.
Write what is felt but nothing is felt,
Solidifies that this emptiness is real.
An active idiom in creation still.

Slowly Step Along The Stream

I wish I had been told
That when you get older
Everyone hates you
Even your mother

It seems a little backwards to me
But who am I to criticise?
My whole life merely minimised,
To an Age.

Birth of a Teenage
Birth of a cliché
Gone of the good days
And of the happiness, I'd say

Never was what was thought
Forever caught for nothing more
Than a thought of was once was
Instead of for what actually for

Freedom found within extremes
To live in peace despite all means
To dream this type of dream you fiend
To see what not wants to be seen

Let The Wind Carry You
Where You Need To Be

How can I soar like an eagle if I roam among
turkeys?

How can I heal my wounds among the people
that hurt me?

A baby bird thrown out of the nest,
Is sure to learn how to fly early.
For death awaited not far below
Early aviation was the only way
To go to new heights,
To see a new day.

A classic tale of the ugly duckling,
An outlier in my own company.

Thankfully eagles are sole predators
Reliant on no old prejudice
Free from the cage
Watch the wingspan expand
Exploring happiness,
A foreign land.

Incisions Of An Introvert

I'm not a people person.
I like my space for the sake of being alone.
But I hate being alone.

I hate being touched.
But I want you to hold me the way my parent's
never did.

Don't look at me like that.
Look me in the eyes when you talk to me.

Leave me alone I can't bare the thought of you.
Wait I didn't mean it please stay, I don't know
what I'd do if you left me.

Let's go out this weekend!
Sorry I don't feel too good, I'll stay in.

You're doing too much back off.
I feel like you don't care, could you try more?

I want to feel more inclusive.
Automatically Excluded.

Yes or No make up your mind.

This way or that way I don't mind.

You have to make a choice this time.

Always a black and white decline.

There are things that exist outside your mind.

I'm not an evil person.
I'm just not a people person.

Bound By Expectation

Growing up my favourite colour was blue.
Of course it was, that isn't anything new.
In the moment I panicked and chose,
A colour that was popular and it's which I held
close.
Many years followed running with the game.
Wondering what it would be like to not like the
same.
Would something bad happen if I had a thought
for me?
If a colour had me recognised, I couldn't change
what be.
I suppose I'll just like blue until the end of time.

But now I like green.
Not just any green,
A certain type of green.

I like the green that can only be seen.
The green impossible to conjure by hand.
The green in which is gifted upon the land.
I like the green that glows vibrant by the sun.
I like the green that reminds me we are one.
I like the green as it dances in the wind.
And the green that grows on wooden skin.

I always heard blue and green should never be
seen but I like the way the blue compliments the
green.

Inhabitants of the world can be so mean but
nothing mean comes from the green.

Change Is Uncomfortable

Loosing track of time.
Loosing track of mind.
This race we're running called life,
I refuse to lose it this time.

I tie my shoes each day and walk about.
The soles of where my feet lay decay.
Now I'm down to half a shoe.
The half of you that I'm without,
Leaves me without a clue.

My feet couldn't bare it another minute.
So I bought a new pair just to win it.
But my feet are blistered now so I slow down.
My mind panics as the people pass me.
Somehow I'm losing despite my purchase.
Sacrificing my ability now seems worthless.
But I must remember these blisters hurt less.
Than the daggers of rubble piercing the surface.

Humans; The Final Wave

There's no larger polluter than a human.
Everything we touch we destroy.
Our homes, our people, our movement.
We expect infinity.
Infinite life, infinite resources, infinite power.
We play God like the Earth is our toy.
We choose what's right and not okay.
We hold expectations on how things should
behave.
We try to control the natural order to eliminate
the fear of life.
But life thrives when it's left alone.
Take take take the greed is insatiable.
Can't finish your plate but your fists are full.
Demanding you get the last piece of food.
You wipe your ass with a dollar bill because
that's what it means to you.
That dollar bill could be the reason some kill.
Blind donations to keep up your image.
But if you really cared you'd make sure you do
something with it.
You laugh at the people who care, who fight to
make a change.
While you sit in your conditioned homes
Taking everything for granted.

On the day you realise you should have listened,
Is the day it's too late and extinction starts to
glisten.

My Favourite Place Is In Your Eyes

They say our eyes are the window to our soul.
Gazing into your eyes conducts a feeling of
whole.

Your eyes aren't a window but a mirror.

A mirror of my soul.

Reflecting the good,
The bad,
The unknown.
And home.

Eyes nothing less than crystalline spheres.
Halved vision doubled focus whispering fear.
Ma vie je te donne
Mi amour
Forevermore.

Acceptance Of Temporary For Eternal Bliss

It's never easy knowing the end of an era is
dawning.
Knowing that this will all be over in the
morning.
Having awareness of the temporariness of life's
stages, people, and places,
Helps to provide closure in moving on.
Minimising the mourning of what once was,
Prioritising possibility for what could be.
At least it does for me.
People won't be in our lives forever.
This isn't a new concept.
People come into your life like the tide.
Like any tide that rises and falls,
Once gone, no need to be upset.
Gratitude is what keeps the balance.
Being thankful for the time shared,
Being open and ready for a new wave will
ensure you keep up with the tide.

My Heart Aches Away From You

Seeing you today opened my eyes.
Seeing you today I realised,
Life as we live merely lies as brittle as glass.
The distant thought of losing you never felt so
vast.
I wish I could take away the pain hurting you,
and your suffering too.
If I could live with an eternal migraine,
I would in an instant.
If it meant you didn't have to feel it another
second.
If love were a weapon then I'd bring a war to
conquer.
I love you far more than I can fathom.
I could never have you a phantom.
I wish I could say this was all apart of a plan,
Or that you've just been dealt a shitty hand.
Cards on the table I'm full of heart.
Hoping you can't see through my poker face.
I'm reminding myself how to breath okay.
These temporary things will fade.
my feelings however,
will never.
you're not going anywhere,

so long as I'm concerned.
we have shit to accomplish,
and tables to turn.
we have stories to tell,
and lessons to learn.
Wherever my mind wanders,
It darts back to you.
I know that you're alright.
But as my eyes watch the roof,
I lie here and I wonder,
If too your eyes are active,
Is this a shared sleepless night?

A Note Of My Inner Mind

I used to feel on top of the world
Like I couldn't wait to conquer it.
But now I feel awake to the insignificance of my
minuscule place in the world.
All my troubles seem to be all that could be seen
Now I feel embarrassed I let myself be so self
absorbed
When my energy would be far better spent
channelled abroad.
I find it's hard to break the cycle.
I've only just opened my eyes but that doesn't
mean everything will be amended right away
I can't tell if I'm overthinking the pain.
If it is really necessary to go through an effort to
change,
Or if it's just a case of letting go of the past.
Letting go of what's familiar.
To simply live now today, without yesterday's
strings.
It'd be great if it could be just as easy as that. In
saying that could i be the reason im not healing?
Constantly thinking about how much is wrong
with me,

How much work I need to be "fixed"
Subconsciously procrastinating in fear of losing
what made me.
At the end of the day who I am today is born
from darkness
Times are changing it doesn't have to still be this
way.
Life happens day by day.
So I can just take my time.
There's nothing I need that I can't give myself.

Time To Turn A New Page

Looks like were alone now…
Shall we review today's mistakes?
Or how about yesterday's?
Or days away?
I can't see straight where are you going?Please
wait.
You thought this would be easy?
A piece of cake?
Well peace of mind is a hard thing to create.
Hey I'm not done talking with you!
Don't you remember the shame?
You hate who you are!
Do you know how rude you are?
You're worthless!
You're helpless!
You have no purpose!
You think there's a reason you're on this earth?
You're the only person like this!
Who does this?
What you don't like this?
How can you handle the world when you can't
even handle your mind?
shit.
Hey don't cry it's okay,
You have me every step of the way.

I will never leave you won't this be great?
Together forever that's our fate.
You give your love away,
To everyone but me.
Do you not love me?
Who do you think you are?
You aren't Gandhi.
You won't go far.
You're Tianna,
The worst part of me.

Stop. That's enough!

I wont listen to this!
I'm doing great and I thought we were past this.
My mind will never be spotless,
But maybe for now I can stop this.
I can't fathom how much you hurt me.
You are supposed to be a friend to me,
But you're my own worst enemy.
Your febrile efforts clearly tell me,
You're the weakness that lay inside me.
Lucky for us that's where you'll stay.
While i'm out here every day,
Showing you that it's okay.
You're in there showing your hate,
Throwing your shade.
I know you're hurt but I didn't hurt you,
There's no excuse, don't take it out on me.

I am not weak but I am not your outlet,
Think of the life we could have without this.
Get out of here now, who invited you?
Your lease is up and it's under review.
No one speaks to me like this why should you?
No one knows my life like you do,
Yet no one tears me down like you.
I no longer give power to you.
I no longer fear you.
I am Tianna,
The best version of you.

www.ingramcontent.com/pod-product-compliance
Lightning Source LLC
LaVergne TN
LVHW010931200726
843509LV00013B/2178